I0469705

Taming Titans

Strategies for Fortune 500 and B2B Relationship Management

Authored by Hugh Garrison

Hugh Garrison

This book is dedicated to the great mentors I have had through the years in the form of customers, friends, teammates, managers and my parents who introduced me to the concepts of business early on.

To my beautiful wife who always supports me in my endeavors.

Most importantly to God and his grace that have allowed me to be so blessed with successes.

Hugh Garrison

Taming Titans: Strategies for Fortune 500 and B2B Relationship Management

I

Hugh Garrison

Taming Titans: Strategies for Fortune 500 and B2B Relationship Management

Introduction

There are many types of selling, and many connotations are associated with this vast vocational spectrum. I would ask you to consider the possibility that we are all salespeople at some point in our job function, and the exploration of techniques and the perspective of experience can help us in many complex business environments. However, for some, sales are our primary career track; we focus on the customer. I'm not talking about the traditional "close the deal and move to the next one in the pipeline." Rather, I refer to the vision of those paramount interactions where corporate messaging and strategy meet the reality of the market. It is the place where sales people become the translators of the company's value and co-biographer of the story. It's where salespeople truly become relationship managers and customer champions to guide the organization to success. This core process, in turn, is what defines the art of relationship selling versus the mechanical step-and-fetch of reciting specs, T-shirt slogans of problems solved by the latest miracle look-alike product, or the limited view of closing a prospect.

Business-to-business (B2B) selling is, by its very nature, a unique world and requires some very different skill sets than what one might think of when looking at sales roles. The greater the company size, scope of the solution, and partnership dollars between two companies, the more the approach becomes "non-sales like" and much more strongly resembles a balanced combination of an advocate-evangelist-advisory-lobbyist role. Throughout this book, we will explore the facets of these types of environments and provide you with some valuable options to consider in your own business development and partnerships.

Hugh Garrison

Taming Titans: Strategies for Fortune 500 and B2B Relationship Management

Among the biggest challenges to creating a masterpiece business relationship between two companies, and not a get-by shadow of what you know your business endeavor can be, are the Titans that stand in our way. Titans can be any number of contentions that manifest as obstacles. Sometimes it may be policies, practices, product issues, or politics that prevent customer success and disconnects between partner companies. These can exhibit themselves as obstacles to goals and progress or team issues that block change. Sometimes it can even be the companies' own cultures clashing.

When we narrow the lens and look at Fortune 500 multinational companies and the dynamics of selling, influencing, and creating long-term partnerships between these giants, we see that Titans of contention tend to be a part of the fabric that weaves the business together. In many ways, the companies themselves can become the Titans wrapped in the relationship that connects them, and we must act to conquer this. In some ways it makes sense, when you consider that most Fortune 500 companies and other large businesses exist to maximize their shareholder value, develop their brand, and create long-term growth through innovation. At the same time, within this construct, companies have to develop corporate partnerships to expand their scope and gain knowledge outside their core competencies without investing in significant human or physical capital.

The opportunities that come from identifying and creating solutions to conquer these Titans are immense and can often define great teams. The amazing thing that I have observed is that when strategic Tier One customers and suppliers find a balance between their corporate metrics and ecosystem partnerships, mutual dependencies can create both synergy and

Hugh Garrison

innovation. As the customer adopts your solution and takes it beyond where your company alone could, returns on investments are only one metric to determine value. From this fertile ground, incredible achievements become the measure of success, and leading industry advancements can even be launched from the combined business-driven union.

My objective is to share with you some proven concepts on constructing a blueprint for strategic Fortune 500 account and relationship management, with the knowledge from the "mistakes and triumph" school of thought. From the fact that you are choosing to invest your time to see another view of the business-to-business spectrum, it is clear you are already an open-minded leader. If indeed you are already in a leadership role between two companies as the customer advocate, these concepts will add to your range of knowledge, making you more effective. You may also be new to customer team leadership or coming from a non-sales perspective; in that case, I hope you will gain some insights to the world of customer relationship management.

Throughout the book we will use really generic examples and analogies to place emphasis on the concepts and practices of relationship management. This technique will prevent debating the merits of product specs or reference to any company in particular. One such reference will be the Magic Widget Company to describe the company that is engaging with the customer and its product. A Widget could be anything from a rocket engine for NASA, or a software application for business analytics. This approach will also allow us to have some fun along the way, as the Magic Widget Company sells some amazing blue Widgets.

Hugh Garrison

Thank you for the opportunity to share these ideas and observations about B2B relationship selling with you. My hope and belief is that they can be harnessed to successfully tame whatever Titans in your business are blocking you from creating your masterpiece.

I wish you much success and good fortune!

Hugh Garrison

Chapter One

Sizing up the situation

We start with creating a system of lenses to explore the world of B2B relationships. There are some critical areas to be aware of, so that you can understand what is movable and what is concrete and can predicatively manage the landscape. As well as adding to your own expertise, this can provide you with another way to see how these core elements intertwine to create the overall account environment.

In some ways, it is the spinning wheel of situational business elements in a six-row business slot machine:

CUSTOMER-TEAM-RELATIONSHIP-MARKET-MECHANISM-PRODUCT

Before we dive into each of these, seeing how they both intertwine and, sometimes, amazingly operate semi independently, I would like to offer you three additional ideas.

Within each of these core variable elements, of the six-row business slot machine resides one of the facets to the larger business puzzle.

These core elements create pillars that hold the business infrastructure in place; where one or more lack the strength to support the fundamental business metrics, the others will expand and exaggerate to compensate. As an example, if you had a very strong strategic relationship, you might be able to overcome a contractual or product issue in the short term (i.e., the relationship pillar would counteract the weaker mechanism and/or market pillar).

Hugh Garrison

These pillars of the business can under go transformation as triggered by one of these six core elements undergoing significant change. In doing so these elements act as a business slot machine, spinning to create a completely new foundation that can be an opportunity or Titian.

Successfully managing the relationship, creating clarity of measures, and removing Titans of contention expose the true potential of the partnership, allowing it to flourish. We will visit these underlying concepts to explore avenues for you to recognize and take advantage of situational events that are creating enough imbalances to pull the lever and reset the core business elements.

Let us continue the journey by defining what each of these six aspects is composed of and how to start evaluating your situation for opportunities.

Customer

As you would expect, it starts with customers and their market position, culture, structure, execution model, and the other underlying framework that creates their corporate identity. In context with the attributes around the core elements, customers relate to their culture and supplier strategy at the top ten level.

Are your customers the market leaders? Do they have the largest opportunity in the market for your product? Or are you the market leader, with the ability to influence the engagement to provide a solution to them to grow their business? Do they have an internal structure that would allow a central organization to manage the supplier base, or is each region or business unit autonomous? Awareness is the idea; no need to

Hugh Garrison

overanalyze it at the moment.

Culture is something very subjective, but it tends to involve things like how they get things done and tactics they take when engaging suppliers. For the most part, as you know from customers of all types, they view supplier relationships within an industry norm, suppliers as part of the solution, pure commodity, or something they must control. If these are their beliefs, then this is out of our scope to effect near term. Knowing we can change their view based on our engagement and setting new standards for the to measure. We just need to be realistic on their position and adjust the elements we can influence. If they view suppliers in the negative sphere, we welcome our first Titan, and we will manage it through the other pillars in our business framework. On a counter and positive front, if your partner customer is a vendor defender, then you have a real opportunity to build trust and accomplish great things sooner.

In either case, our job right now is to identify what your customer's stance is toward suppliers, and we will work through the core elements to complete view of our ecosystem.

Teams

With every large customer and company selling the dream Widget, there is a vast scope of relationship bridging the chasm. A theoretical corresponding sales model and team fit like a tailored suit, at least in theory. The tailored fit would have the perfect team, a great corresponding customer leadership, a fantastic product, an ideal contract, and the feeling as if you are wearing comfortable pajamas. Of course, reality may look a bit different than the ideal state referenced or our prefect fit. This might take the form of something such as product issue, customer access, contract boundaries, or other looming Titans. That always feels like that nagging tag inside your shirt that rubs your back all day and that is our opportunity.

First, we need to understand if the team in place interacts well with the customer, or if there is an overabundance of strife in the basic mechanics of working with the customer. If you've been in the lead role, you know this already; if not, look for those telltale signs of over positioning little things, multiple requests to get simple data, or lack of respect about the customer when facing internally.

Second, how does the internal organization view our team? Does the team have credibility and influence with key stakeholders? Alternatively, are they tolerated as the current customer interface? As the leader, if the internal stakeholders are pulling you into tactical decision-making tiebreakers multiple times on the same issue that is a clear sign the team is suffering some image problems. If your team is asking you for help, that could be a good thing, as they want to ensure everyone is in alignment. Balance of communication, delegation, and taking direct action are the challenges we face.

Third, we have to observe and make a judgment call on how the team interacts together. As we will see further in the journey of taming Titans, large, cross-functional, extended teams are the nature of Fortune 500 B2B relationships. In this phase, we need to get a gut feel for whether or not the team gets along and works as one, or there is contention.

Finally, we need to take inventory on skill sets of your team based on your industry norms. One of the best things about managing, leading, and being a part of large B2B teams is that you get to interact with the majority of functions in your company—and, many times, the customers. Sometimes this means that you have people reporting to you who are outside of your area of core knowledge. Of course, you cannot be an expert in all fields—and frankly, I think if you focus too much on one discipline, your ability to discern the balanced approach wanes somewhat. Here is an example to keep in mind: Although I am not a welder, I do understand the importance of strong welds and tested processes to ensure the side of my car does not fall off. One of the things I have done over the years is to build a network of functional experts, whom I can call to help me with judgments on team functions outside my area of expertise. Your conclusion needs to allow you to discern if the core team of contributors has the necessary industry and functional skills needed.

Relationship

With a high-level view of your team, let us look at the element of relationship of our B2B landscape. There are many similarities between all B2B selling environments. However, the size of the enterprises directly creates the complexity and scope of what you have to manage. If you are climbing Mount Everest, as opposed to a day hike to your local park, it is a very different experience. You would look silly for you to swing your kids at the park wearing full gear and climbing spikes, just like it would probably end badly for you if you were wearing shorts and flip-flops at even the base camp on Everest.

The way I view it is as a formula. Please do not worry, I am not an engineer, and I don't play one at work. The formula is this: your company's size and scope of business + your customer's size and scope = ERS (entire relationship spectrum). With this as our guideline, what is your entire relationship spectrum? Is it supplier to customer only, or are you a multinational

Hugh Garrison

company with $10 billion annual revenues selling to a $400 million distributor? Alternatively, are you co-designing technology solutions that end up at Best Buy, with both logos on the product and the thousand or so interactions that occur before the product hits the shelves? Maybe you're responding to RFQ data only at this point, and the objective is to get on an approved vendor list. Even more exciting is that you're building a path to adoption of your product solution inside the customer's enterprise. The counterview is that you or your customer is extremely askew, and this drives a one-sided rule. If you're a $5M private company in an open market, and your customer is a $50B giant, things will be very skewed in the customer's favor. Whatever the entire scope of the mutual business interactions and dependencies is, that is the framework of the relationship that is our baseline.

Market

In this characteristic, we want to identify the basic marketplace and each of the company's positions within it, as well as the industry conditions that influence the specific market. In other words, understand the business environment in which your customers must compete. In this discovery you will find a multitude of avenues to understand your solution's full potential and how to articulate that in the form of value.

Once that is well understood, it will play a role in how we solve our problems of Titans that block our overall progress. Just one example would be if your managing a customer in a market that has twenty suppliers of the Magic Widgets, versus in one that has five; it's going to change the scope of the relationship and other elements. I believe that, although it can be counterintuitive sometimes, the bigger the market space and fewer Magic Widget players, the more complex and challenging the environment. Think of it as a closed or limited market, which creates a finite ecosystem that you and your customer live in. You have to deal with a legacy of installed products, both yours and your competitors', which creates both opportunities and potential barriers to entry.

Mechanism

This is probably the most binary of the elements, and it sometimes holds some valuable jewels we will want to mine. In the simplest form, this includes the contracts, workflows, business practices, common processes, forums, and any other mechanism that allows product, money, and development to flow between the companies. Titans of contention live here, too, as it brings forth some seemingly unchangeable aspects of the B2B environment. If the master contract between the companies states that there is a 5 percent charge to all returns found not defective, that could massively impact the business, if we are selling two million Magic Widgets per quarter at $390 each, and your return rate just spiked 20 percent. Another binary switch is that our solution either is or is not approved within the customer's systematic mechanism for acquisition of our category. Either of these creates events that, depending on the vision you have for your business, might trigger a reset to the core pillars of the business.

Product

For our purposes, we want to understand our product reality. If what we are selling is incredibly great and game changing, then we are extremely fortunate and can open doors to gain access to many levels of the customer by product alone It doesn't ensure success, though—that's where the skills, strategy, and know-how of Taming Titans gives us an advantage. The next step is to baseline your product across four viewpoints: innovation appeal (by selecting our Widget,

Hugh Garrison

does the customer have a chance to gain internal or external credibility or value creation?), total cost of ownership or ROI (depending on product), ecosystem bandwidth (the size of adjoining or integrated value add associations), and customer or market specific requirements (does our product or device meet an industry requirement?).

Once the business slot machine of CUSTOMER-TEAM-RELATIONSHIP-MARKET-MECHANISM-PRODUCT has spun in any given situation and combination, these elements become the pillars of our business environment. Some become the Titans we must deal with; others will be devices of strength that will enable us to overcome obstacles to create our masterpiece. As with any work of art, that unique vantage point is in the beholder's eyes—or, in our case, the leaders. Properly articulating these concepts to your customers and your internal organization will allow you to gain the most progress and creatively find balanced solutions. Your solutions may be revenue achievement, strategic engagement that leads to joint product wins, or successful adaptation of a new business model and team structure. Whatever the view is after accessing the landscape of where you are across the core elements, this will make an extremely powerful foundation of understanding to launch the concepts we discover on the rest of our journey.

Major Points and Insight

To better understand the B2B environment we are in we can create a system of lenses to help view and define the situation

The main definitions are; CUSTOMER-TEAM-RELATIONSHIP-MARKET-MECHANISM-PRODUCT

These core elements create pillars that hold the business

Hugh Garrison

infrastructure in place and as one changes position it is like that of a business slot machine, as each effects the other to some degree. Understanding the core elements is critical and each has it's own set of learning's.

It's important to review each element to give it clarity and understand its purpose. First, the customer needs to be defined by their market position, culture, structure and execution model, to make visible their corporate identity. The customer team needs to be reviewed to ensure they have the skills, internal and customer relationships, team chemistry and know how to solve the current environment created by the core elements positions The Relationship needs to be scoped to understand the mutual interactions and common bonds between the two companies.

We can then turn more outward, determining what the larger market and ecosystem that the companies operate within. Then we can follow the value chain with the final solution that reaches the end customer. This can be fully vetted out by visualizing the mechanism that allows the companies work together and reality of the product being transacted across the B2B relationship.

It is through successfully managing the relationship, creating clarity of measures, and removing Titans of contention that we expose the true potential of the partnership and allow it to flourish.

Hugh Garrison

Chapter Two

Arranged Marriages

I often think that B2B relationships present some truly unusual situations that, from the outside, look as though they would create the easiest of selling environments. However, sometimes, when we are in the middle of a closed or limited market loop, the question is not, "Will they buy from us?" but rather, "How do we gain trust and enable the overall relationship to flourish and thus create long-term mutual revenue and innovation?" A closed or limited market is where the supplier base for some product or technology reason is finite, due to market conditions. This limited condition may be due to market size, technology or raw materials access, competitive offering, or specialized adaptation. In addition, there may be extremely high barriers to entry and long lead times on specialized product offerings. Maybe it is a software or application that is propriety or system specific. Whatever the condition, it creates limitations to the access. For commodities, this essentially creates a condition that takes nearly all suppliers to meet the majority of demand in the market most of the time. The other condition that could create a limited business market is the size of the customer. If a customer is big enough to consume 20 percent or more of the total market, then the ecosystem will behave like a limited market. Finally, this condition could exist if the product, technology, or service provided within the ecosystem is unique enough that there is no true substitute. Such conditions can create an "arranged marriage" of sorts; companies become locked into a business relationship potentially based on a "must have" situation. Contrast this with a full or open market condition, where multiple near-identical-solution suppliers are producing more than the market needs.

Hugh Garrison

As you are probably aware, a more open market and ecosystem finds a more traditional sales approach, which is about filling the "funnel" or "pipe" with prospects and deals— knowing some will close, and some will not. However, without a steady pipeline of activity, it is hard to survive long term. There are certainly some very valuable lessons we can learn from experiencing this type of sales model, such as discipline of process, customer interface skills, proposal preparation, and contact management.

The consumer-based model is probably furthest away from the large B2B model. It is extremely transactional and is influenced by demographics and popular culture. Naturally, many of the Fortune 500 companies are retail and consumer-focused. However, many operate in limited ecosystems behind the firewall of their internal operations and supply chain.

The framing of the limited B2B environment is something we needed to establish in order to further our journey on how to manage this landscape successfully. So here we are in a limited ecosystem and market; the customer has to do some level of business with us, and life must be good, right? It is certainly a good place to be, with the opportunity to make a difference, creating some truly incredible revenue and team milestones along the way. This moment of realization is where we have our arranged marriage of sorts, one in which our customers almost have to buy something from us in the limited ecosystem or closed market; and we can create a foundation of trust, long-term growth, and amazing innovation.

In order to create, we must be aware. I am betting you are reading this book, not merely to pass the time, but to add some knowledge to your intellectual arsenal to solve problems

Hugh Garrison

and increase your success. You are already receptive to new ideas in the fact you're reading a book to expand your view. So we just need to make the uniqueness of a limited-environment B2B model very visible. Understanding some basic constructs will create our foundation to enable growth and innovation, while building our Titan defense system. There are many parts to a successful B2B relationship; however, these are the ones connected within and around our customer's organization and systems of measure to frame the overall landscape. The ones we will investigate are cycle time, competitive landscape, our company's organization; customers' groups, and go-to-market model.

Cycle time

In most cases, time becomes something that we have to measure in blocks of events. This means that the typical cycle is probably quarterly, with RFQs, normal tactical business reviews and futures planning meetings. We need to make a clear timeline of these and create a map of when what is. As the leader of the account, we get to have access to all meetings. These planned engagements give us both insights for our company and the opportunity to present out to our customers on whatever the topic; it is also gives the company's executives better understanding of our customers. Regardless of whether the meetings are in our functional area or not, this is extremely powerful; and if managed as a roadmap of how to engage our customers, we can gain knowledge, effective communication, and position information outside our normal channels. However, given the nature of our limited market ecosystem, things happen that can offset everything else. If our Magic Widgets uses compound X, and it is in a region that just got a new king that says no compound leaves the kingdom without his approval…things are going to slow down and affect the industry. In this case, event timing

Hugh Garrison

will overrule our normal cycle times, creating some disruption. Remember the core elements we discussed in chapter 1? This example would be a Market Element trigger that could spin the other elements in different ways. This can be a good thing and can allow our industry to take the spotlight, as the limited market will become constrained. We can use this as an opportunity to gain access to other functional areas our customer and develop a better understanding of your industry.

As you manage major events and their effects on your customer, you need to realize balance will return. With this in mind, planning for the natural timing of cycles in your customer's business, you can map out the flow of engagements to create a well-rounded approach to introduce new concepts, place future markers, and secure allies in your quest to create a masterful customer relationship.

Competitive landscape

There are multitudes of ways to look at competition. I will try to influence you to view it in this regard: be aware of the competition in your industry and local market, and stop short of talking to or associating with competitors who do business on your customers. Of course, it is important to understand what offerings they have and their advantages from a quality, technology, attribute solutions, or supply chain perspective. You will need to scope out the total number of competitors and the position each has at your account. Usually, in large B2B relationships this is open knowledge and part of the business metrics review quarterly. If not, just ask your trusted procurement or business group leader, and they will more often than not share a wealth of data with you, if you are a trusted supplier. One of the biggest reasons to be independent is that no matter what you learn from your competitor, it provides nothing we can use with our customer. Trust me

Hugh Garrison

when I tell you, any procurement or business group leader can see you coming a mile away by the questions you are asking, and if your knowledge is outside your company's view, it will be damaging for you. As this is important, we will talk more on this in the future chapters; you can only negotiate internally with the delegation given by your customer, not your competition. Once you understand this part of the ecosystem, we can turn our attention to our company and some ideas on potentially interacting with our customer to bring both value and access.

Magic Widget Company Organization

It is imperative to comprehend the company's organization to discover how to accomplish tactical and strategic efforts. Just as critical is clearly seeing the customer model and the axis it turns on in the form of how decisions are made. The approach is to be cognizant of groups outside our organization; let's make the assumption that we can marshal our resources in our own group. As you might guess—or perhaps have already experienced—one's own company can itself be the biggest Titan to manage. If we take an imaginary divide, one edge of the canyon is our company, and the other is our customer. On the company side, let us get five groups identified and mapped out. Business units, executive management, supply chain, finance, and factory/production planning or development group are the people we want to influence and create a network with, which we can use to start to build the bridge over to our customers. We purposely did not include the groups we would directly manage, such as account managers, salespeople, field teams, and other customer-facing folks; we'll get to them in the next chapter. The title of the organizations outside our immediate span of control may be a bit different, but it is the function they serve that we need to focus on. We need to appreciate what is driving our core business units, the teams responsible for the P and L of the company, is that market share or margin or unit growth etc. The next group to look at is the executive management. I am talking about the C-level offices—are they of the mind-set that being involved directly with the customer is good, or are they more of a corporate, focused group that prefers to manage from a distance? As we move to supply chain, we want to be very aware of how the complete forward and reverse logistics work and how our sub supplier strategy is managed. We must take into account our finance groups; we need to be able to confirm who has what delegation on deals, long-term pricing, and tactical financial mechanics. This might look like credits for returns, erosion quarter over quarter, rebate structures, and other incentives to influence demand. Finally, we need to be clear on who allocates product and determines future commitments for the product going to the customer. In the case of software or services, we want to know who is putting priority on what projects and controlling the output of new generations. With all of these core groups understood, it will be more visible what and whom we want to pull into engagement with our customers, to help educate and influence them.

Customer Groups and Go to Market Model
On the other side of the canyon, let us lay out the primary customer groups to which we will be building the bridge and finishing the construction. How do they take our product to market within their solution? What is their core value to the market? Are we the primary component and jointly developed, or are we a faceless SKU in the bill of materials? No matter our calling inside their solution, in most of the cases, a procurement organization acts as a primary relationship and interface conduit. We need to understand who makes the final call and how they award business, meaning what are their fundamentals—such as price, supply, product features, and so

Hugh Garrison

on. The next groups to seek are the marketing and business units. These groups determine their solution's offering and how the value stack is weighted to place the importance on each of the components in their final solution. As we look at our specific Widget, if it's physical then we need to integrate ourselves with the supply chain and operations groups. If it's a service or software, then fully vetting out the development teams and architect leaders is critical. Lastly, we need to get visibility to the executive level to understand who makes the decisions and why they integrate outside products (might be software, components or service) from a strategic and needs perspective. With both sides of the relationship canyon understood, we can start to work on uniting the two, with a bridge connecting the common groups.

We have sized up the overall situation in chapter 1 to see more clearly where our relationship fits within the five elements of Customer, Teams, Relationship, Market, and Mechanism. Now that we have reviewed the nature of large Tier 1 suppliers and identified the customer landscape, with regard to functions within both organizations, we need to recognize understand how to influence and begin to mold the business situation into our vision of success. The art of this type of business endeavor becomes how to make the process effortless, as the companies execute to common goals, cultivating the relationship to be an innovation and growth engine, not getting the "sale"…that part has already done. Making the transition to this type of relationship management is not always easy, but to try to apply traditional sales tactics would be like bringing a baseball bat to paint your masterpiece. Something would surely happen; however, the results would be very messy and probably not wanted.

Major Points and Insight

Business-to-business relationships are created out of a need for a company to extend beyond it's core competencies or gain product or market availably from outside sources to complete it's own solution, There are two basics market principles, a closed or limited market there the supplier base for some product or technology reason is finite or an open market that has extended ecosystem and commoditized availability.

The concept of cycle times with customer or internal repeated events or forums is key to creating opportunities to accomplish goals to further our vision.

Understanding the competitive landscape is extremely important, but should be handle with caution.

Creating a map of sorts to navigate both our company's and the customers' organization and how they interact will help to understand who the key stakeholders are and how to influence them. To fully utilize the knowledge of our company to solve customer problems, we need to operate with the delegation grated to us by our customer. This is where the reality sets in that the larger the Tier 1 customer-to-supplier relationship is, the more need to manage in a non-sales-type manner.

Hugh Garrison

Chapter Three

It Takes an Army

I've always been a car enthusiast. From the first car I customized to the first car I bought from the dealership showroom—they each held mystery. The fact that you have three or four thousand pounds of metal (nowadays, plastic too) moving fast, through all the many mechanical parts and pieces under the hood and throughout the vehicle, is pretty amazing. Think about the spark plug igniting, sending the piston down, and turning the cam that pushes the valves to all work as one unit called an engine. Then the clutch engages and puts the transmission in gear, to turn the driveshaft and spin the wheels. When you're ready to slow down and stop, you downshift and apply the brakes. All these mechanical parts, a working as one, make the car go and does what is designed to do. . If one part doesn't work or is out of time with the others, life is not so good. The goal is to keep the car well maintained, to ensure it can perform at its maximum capability.

Like cars, teams have many moving parts, and if not all are working together in the same direction, there may be some really disastrous effects. The larger and more complex the business partnership, the larger the team and process scope needed to manage it. The comparison to our car example would a semi truck carrying hydrogen versus a tiny car that seats two. They both move down the road, but they take an entirely different level effort to do so and serve very different purposes. Our efforts will focus more on how to manage the semi truck carrying hydrogen and how to make it perform its intended purpose of delivery high-value material to its destination as effectively and quickly as possible, without blowing anything up. To do that, we are going to need lots of people who are experts on everything from turbo-charged diesel engines to managing explosive compounds and processes that align it all.

How should our team strategy be arranged and focused to bring the most benefit to the situation and not blow something up unintentionally? As we discussed briefly in chapter 2, identifying the functional groups outside our own customer team is an important step. The next step is to lay out in our minds the scope of our direct and indirect teams. This might look like engineers, developers, marketing, or service people, who face the customers, and our role as the team leader allows us direction with these resources. The essence is that there is a wide spectrum of divisions and people within a company who are necessary to take the R&D of Magic Widgets all the way to consumption of the end widget by our customers. In most multinational companies, it can be likened to an army, as the support teams are divided into core units, each of which performs a part of the war effort, while being directed at the strategic level by the generals. In a company's case, it's the CEO and his or her staff who act as the common point for the strategy that will be disseminated to the troops, and each functional unit will execute its part of the overall strategy. Let's dive in now and explore some concepts to manage both the expanded customer team and all the functional teams to be successful.

Now that the idea of our army is in place, we need to establish some sense of order and common objectives. Let's look back at the situational business elements: CUSTOMER-TEAMS-RELATIONSHIP-MARKET-MECHANISM-PRODUCT. We can take *customer* and *mechanism* and then figure what our customer requires from our corporate army and the mechanisms we need to execute. The basic customer reality is what, how, and where our product will be integrated in the final solution provided by our customer to the market. These product, solution, or customer requirements become the singular direction for engagements and the guideposts for your deployment of corporate resources. Compare this to driving only your company's agenda, viewing direction from your customers vantage point will ensure balance. Balance is absolutely critical to long-standing customer success. Anything can exist in an unbalanced way for a short period of time, in recognizing when things are lopsided can be a great opportunity. For this line of reasoning, we need to make the assumption that our Magic Widgets are critical to the customer's solutions, like tires to a car. Continuing down this path toward, what product or service are we providing? This simple question is not only the foundation of our relationship; it can be the most complex question, depending on what the interdependencies around what our Magic Widget does. There could also be a larger ecosystem of assisting products, services, technologies, or hosts that may be needed to enable our complete solution to reach it's full potential.

From a product or service Widget perspective, we will have people in our army who research, design, build, or code programs, manage the logistics and finance aspects We need to identify who the lieutenants are in each of these critical functions of the customer engagement cycle. Then we need to turn to our customer and understand the mechanisms that govern the engagement. There will be three different time zones for your Magic Widget: past, present, and future. The past will be about things happening to products that have already made it to their final destination or services already rendered. The present will be the aspect of what we are doing this cycle—the latest revenue, projects underway, and other aspects of real-time business. The future state is what we are planning with our customers in the form of joint plans or future integration of our Magic Widgets with the customer. It can also be future Widget plans or technology that are not present in the current Widget.

Just like a battle plan, we need to identify the landscape and match up our internal battalions to the customer's needs or product engagements. The war we are fighting is not with the customer but with the Titans we face to move our business forward. By facing them, finding ways to overcome the Titan, the value is created and can come through in every engagement between the companies. We cannot be everywhere at once, of course, and this is why we have the army to support us. In a past example, we might have a widget provided that was not 100 percent complete and now our quality or field services teams are going to be needed. We orchestrate the actions or call the air strike. By using the customer's processes as bookends, direction for the functional teams is clear, and everyone is moving in the same direction. Current product battles may look like cost pressures on the business, due to market dynamics outside of our control, weak demand, or some new Widget coming soon. Knowing the right battalion (i.e.: what team) and who makes the decisions will allow us to get the army moving toward the help we need. A future product engagement would be the troops that are developing new Widgets, and we call them in to help establish what the future will look like and how the two companies can shape a part of it. With the product understood and all time slots covered, we want to turn our attention to mechanisms that are available to us.

More than likely, the companies will have established forums to address the product in all three time slots—past, present, and future. We will need to identify each as it relates to your

Magic Widget. If we are shipping a product, then there will be monthly or quarterly reviews on integration and field data, as both companies will track these metrics. A Titan that lives in this time zone is always a field issue; perhaps somehow our Magic Widgets didn't perform as expected in the field. Now our business is being impacted, and/or our customer is coming to us for relief of some kind. We should apply the theory of directing the army to perform triage and drop troops behind enemy lines, so to speak. A very powerful approach is to have the experts directly engage the customer's experts, step back, and allow them to mutually solve the issue. We can't scale our business or customer relationship if we feel the need to be in every conversation and engagement. As the customer leader, we have the right to ask both companies for a forum, if one does not already exist, and have the functional teams report back to us on the progress and brief us on next steps. The same is true of the future mechanisms as well. Chances are, our customer has its own army of people performing task and developing solutions for their customers.
Development engineers and product solution experts lead the way to the forum; allow these groups to work together to solve issues.

The present time zone for your product is probably where we will have our direct and indirect team engage the most. This time zone is where the revenue plan comes together, and we probably have the most influence to affect the results. The teams responsible for product inventories and/or integration management will be critical to influence. Also, the production part of the company will ensure we have the product pipe full and opportunity gets fulfilled. The sales cycle of negotiating how many Widgets and how much value the customer places on them in the form of pricing is, of course, a main ever in the current time zone. Again, taking the approach that we are

Hugh Garrison

deploying resources and tactics to fit the current space will allow us the scale to manage extremely complex and significant revenue.

The company's lieutenants, the sales mangers or reps who work for us directly, need to have clear guidance and expectations for how to run the business. I would offer the viewpoint that the sales leads for either the customer or, if the relationship is large enough, the segment itself, are at the middle of the functional matrix to guide the direction. This is where the cross-functional teams must be tied together by the common customer goals. The creativity of the leader and the team can really be expressed in this process, fitting the company's agenda into the confines of the customer's mechanisms and vision. This exercise alone will provide insight into both companies' strategies as we work to aggregate across the Tier 1 supplier-customer relationship. This is the planning stage and a natural engagement to build strategies for the future. Ideally, it is a mutual exercise. If not, we can overcome this Titan by being an expert on our customer's business and market and creating ideas that solve problems facing the customer and market growth. This gives us the forum and collateral to have meetings with the customer to explore these possibilities. We can change the course of the war of customer collaboration by changing the time frame we talk about in a given event. The future is yet to be written, and by its fluid nature, it creates a mutual tone that allows for a natural dialogue of coaction.

As we define the overall direction, two key elements that will need to be incorporated into our overall battle plan are the core role deliverables for each position on the team—who owns what. Then, establish standard processes to manage the day-to-day operations. We'll see this idea again when we

Hugh Garrison

review our vision; one effective way to do this is to develop a RASCI (a format of responsibility that depicts who is Responsible, Accountable, Supportive Consulted, and Informed for the task).

Remember our pillars of business, the core elements? When something changes, it can shift the balance, we are in an incredible position as this happens. The value we bring as leaders of the customer team is to match the right resources to the situation. This is the birthplace of strategy and the tactics to execute the vision as we see the landscape change. The other critical part is giving on-the-ground feedback to our company. This means that, our team leaders and our core customer team have the clearest view to offer potential solutions, unrealized opportunities, and quantify risk to a given event or situation. In essence, the strategy that you need to devise takes your direct relationship with the customer and places the functional groups surrounding your team next to the customer's functional experts to create synergy and scale. Thinking of these resources as an army to deploy, one whose deployment can be influenced by our direct team, will help you think in larger scale. What we probably know, if we are leading a global team between two major companies, and the concept we are trying to get across is that we have to figure out the best way to call our army of resources to action. We know that we cannot be experts in all the functional areas, or be physically everywhere all the time. Finally, the concept that there are product time zones, defined as past, present, and future teams, with accountability by task, will help drive efficiencies. In addition, seeing things in time zones will help separate engagements, and what functional teams we need to have deployed to help solve crisis, execute to revenue goals and build a path to sustained success.

Hugh Garrison

Major Points and Insight

Like complex mechanical cars, cross-functional customer teams have many moving parts that we must pay attention to in order to have everyone moving in the same direction.

When working with and managing large functional teams, seeing them as an army to be deployed to different fronts to solve problems based on their unique skills is good way to bring clarity of purpose. Always remember, that the war we are fighting is not about the customer, but the Titans we face to move our business forward.

As Titans emerge, we need to ensure we are managing all the events in the right time zones of past, present, and future to put the right frame of reference forward. For example, we can often change the course by changing the time frame you talk about. The future is yet to be written and by it's fluid nature, it creates a mutual positive tone that allows for a natural dialog of coaction even in the worst of tactical crisis.

As we go through these processes and move our business to the next plateau, the team's creativity can really be expressed through fitting the company's goals into the confines of the customer's mechanisms and vision. This is where the cross-functional teams must be tied together by a common leadership voice and direction.

Hugh Garrison

Chapter 4

Transparency Always

When I think of transparency, I think of it as a way of conducting myself in the business realm that promotes clear communication around what my agenda is. It's about transmitting information in a way that is useful and relevant to the intended audience. Let's face it, information in the form of data—well, there is an abundance of that all around us via any given portal. Hence, information in itself is not power; knowledge and awareness are, however, powerful. How we interpret knowledge, package it, and then present the information is critical. For our purpose of working through the practice of being transparent in our overall business relationships, we can think of a presentation where all sides are the same—customer, company, and team. Creating the mechanisms that produce that level of openness is the challenge and core part of managing B2B landscapes.

There are many ways to engage the customer in a B2B environment; the simplest and most long-term-focused approach is transparency. I love the concept of the "closer" or "hunter"; it works really well in direct selling, when we are trying to reach a very finite, short-term goal. However, in the world of most sizable B2B customer relationships, we have to be able to look out well into the future and understand that there is many opportunities to present, collaborate, and move mutual goals to the next level. There are rarely the big "close" or "get the order" moments; so it takes a different approach, skill set, and personality to be successful. There are of course critical events within the five core elements that create opportunities to create a shift in the status quo or intervene to enable change. It is a progression of both strategic and

Hugh Garrison

tactical maneuvers that creates lasting positive effects to grow the mutual business. Hence, being transparent in our engagements and each step of influencing both the customer and our own company's stakeholder's makes for a much more productive and sustained progression. As we work across the matrix organization, having both constancy of message and measure is like the engine that powers the ship to the destination of our choosing. Besides, if we are constantly trying to manipulate and use spectacular counterintelligence to get your objectives achieved, it will be apparent to the smart folks we're trying to influence. More damaging, we could win doing the "different message to each person" approach to manipulate people, but in doing so, the situation will probably go around in circles and then stop, as the stories collide at some eventual point.

A few basic rules on transparency: there is not one of these that are more critical than the others, as they all work in unison. Nothing about being transparent removes the inherent responsibility of being a good steward of our company and protector of confidential information that gives the Magic Widget Company its market advantage.

If we look at some the core areas of transparency, as it relates to engagements with our customer and all the stakeholders in the Magic Widget Company, we find that mechanism, market events, issues, information, and objectives are all intertwined. Beyond the contract and business practices, market events, and all other business goings-on, there is an incredible opportunity for creativity, and it can be a strong weapon against the Titans of contention. The Titans are created with stifled information and cumbersome process that have long ago drowned in the wasteland of "we've always done it this way," or "this is how Magic Widget Company and super

Hugh Garrison

customer work." As we look at each of the core areas were we need transparency, we'll give some examples of creative ways to manage a sometimes-stale process by opening a window of light, so that all the smart people involved in the relationship can contribute. By doing so, I am convinced your own very bright, creative mind will explore ways for you to adapt ways to be transparent and bring more creativity to your business success.

When we are looking for opportunities to find avenues to bring more value that sometimes resides both a Titan of contention as well as stale process, is the formal contract between the two companies. There is more than likely an overriding contract or set of business rules that governs the formal relationship and sets the boundaries for interactions between two large commercial partners. This guideline carves out the tactical and business expectation and is the mechanism that drives the business. If we are coming into a leadership role on a customer team, this will give us a good platform to look and observe what is being practiced versus what is in the contract. The opportunity is to be able to convey the parameters of the mundane contract into conditions that create both predictability and constancy. Although this may be putting you to sleep, don't underestimate the influence you can have with predicable, consistent results. The market rewards these attributes; and honestly, your team will look like heroes every time. What's the end game? Be open about what the contract between the two companies is and how the business is or is not operating to those standards. If you see areas you want to move the current practice back to the contract vs. current state, be up front with that perspective and listen to the feedback you get; the insight you gain might be surprising.

A seemingly simple, but sometimes very involved process,

Hugh Garrison

creative way to approach the central mechanism is to create a one-page "standard process guidelines" document. If there is a fifty-page contract, get with your legal and business partners inside the company and uncover the essentials to the operational mechanics. The customer leader or your team may initially react oddly to the idea that you are bringing what will seem like rules to a process they have been using for a while. Here is the deal: it's business, and rules and measures are how it works. The more open these are, the better off you will be, as more trust and credibility will be developed when you demonstrate you clearly understand the foundation. Opportunities are crated when you change and/or modify the process or contract to suite the best practices and new dynamics of a changing macro environment. This can be really useful when you are trying to work an issue with a non–customer-facing group, and you need to get closure. Let's say you are trying to get freight expedited or new coding done inside a very narrow window of time. The answer from your internal stakeholders is that you are twentieth in line, and it will be well outside of what you need and have committed to as a solution.

One way to take advantage of the formal contract to break this Titan is that you can ask, "do one through nineteen have a contract that will be broken or other agreement that will be shattered if we don't execute? " You can adapt this, of course, to fit the situation and level of pressure you want to apply. The takeaway is that if the contract and/or formal process that govern your business relationship are not known—or, worse, are a corporate a myth—it does no good in helping you be successful to achieve both customer and your goals. In fact, it can create a Titan of smoke and mirrors. Simple discipline, through application of transparency and understanding, using your creativity to paint a scene, as you want, can condemn the Titans of contention.

Hugh Garrison

Like the weather in Texas, market events can change in an instant and can have a dramatic effect on the business landscape. This can range from consolidation of suppliers and/or customers to technology or demand shifts that fundamentally change the value propositions across the board. The idea here is that once an event has happened, don't wait for your customer to tell you about it, if at all possible.

Obviously, if the event involves your Magic Widget Company, then you get to abide by the rules in place around the event— maybe a merger or new market opening up. However, most of the time your company is aware, as are you, so being alert to market conditions and changes is critical. As the leader of the customer team, you need to proactively turn inside and seek the company's position on the event. This has many side benefits as well. One is that you might choose to delegate this to one of your leaders, to gather facts to form the message. This creates trust and encourages your team to grow. The other positive effect is that your customers will be able to use this data to educate their internal stakeholders. This not only creates that trusted relationship with the customer, it allows your team to be viewed as the source for industry data. There is not a clearer example of a multilateral win.

One way to weave an open, creative approach to the business mechanisms is to create common or internal central dashboards. You could think about the business like a sporting event that people (your extended teams and non–customer-facing people) are watching, trying to follow the key scores and important landmarks. The most efficient way to provide information is being consistent and show the high level situation, so everyone can get orientated to what's going on.

Hugh Garrison

Begin with the core Widgets you are managing, and then apply the measures that are important to your success. For example, if shipping a million of blue Widget #12 is the goal, and you're at six million to date, you could have a speedometer showing 1.5m (room to overachieve) and starting speed of zero, the needle on 6. You can make these graphic depictions as comprehensive as you want. However, keep in mind, this real time update is quick view for business health and progress conditions, not a novel. So if you can keep it to one or two pages that will make it more powerful. The next step is to have weekly or monthly update using your high-level business overview; the cadence of your business cycle will determine the frequency, updates with your leadership teams. Once you have the internal version built out, show it your customer leader; get their buy in and feedback. In doing this, you'll find common objectives and agenda, allowing for the power of your mutual organization to work. The purpose is to create transparency, and the customer will probably have input and ideas. One of the key values this can provide you are a forum of your creation to review the areas of the account you feel are important with the stakeholders and executive leaders on both sides of the equation. The other aspect is that it creates very clear expectations and common actions.

Issues—we all have them. The best-run companies have problems with programs and products; it's what makes some of the best opportunities to build trust. Strong relationships are not built on wine and roses, but rather on the tribulation of events faced together. As we've talked about in most Tier 1 relationships, the value realized by your customer is taking your product and integrating it into an end-user solution. This creates a unique alliance, one where your Magic Widget may impact the end customer through your customer. Tensions can

Hugh Garrison

run high, as there are multiple layers of communication and resolution management. The bright side of pending disaster is that you can establish credibility as the customer or event expert through being the leader who steps forward with the initial information or position. This might look like the one who goes to the customer or internal stakeholder with the news that the blue Widgets were produced as yellow, shipped out into the field, and now our customer is wanting them replaced. This is where knowing who does what and being collaborative with the internal leaders will pay dividends. Once you have creatively produced a customer-facing template—one that speaks in the customers' language, so that they can in turn transmit the issue to their teams—you can start the process. Experience says it is a good idea to get the key customer leaders together and brief them on the high-level issues before you start your campaign. This allows you to frame the issues and act as the trusted advisor on what their options are, as you have the agreed to internal delegation to talk to the facts available. In this process, you can get their feedback on how to tweak further communication to them in a way that will be most valuable. The main thing is that you want to establish a trusted link between your internal teams and customers on issues, so that you can create transparent conduit of information. This will allow for much faster problem solving than trying to fake it or position every part of the information or answer and in the end will lead to a much better relationship.

Throughout the discussion of transparency, we have called out the concept that our company's vision and, in turn, specific objectives need to be out in the open, to create the highest levels of engagement, creating common forms of governing. Metrics and visible measures are a very real way to navigate the complexity of multinational account management. Finding the approach that works for you, whether an overall

Hugh Garrison

dashboard, standard operational guidelines, or other vehicles to transmit the metrics and issues to the customers, team, and internal stakeholders is critical.

Major Points and Insight

Transparency is a way of conducting ourselves in the business realm that promotes clear communication around our agenda and transmitting information in a way that is useful and relevant to our intended audience.

While we are surrounded by information, knowledge and awareness are how we interpret that information. In our B2B universe, information is about our business state with our customer and strategy to accomplish our vision. Value is derived when we create, package and present the information in a way that is relevant. The most efficient way to provide information is be consistent so everyone can get orientated to what's going on. A tactic to accomplish this is creating a one-page "standard process guidelines" document, outlining all the relevant and practical processes that the business operates. In addition, developing common central dashboards to create a map that people (our extended teams and non–customer-facing people) can use to follow the business key scores and important relationship landmarks is also vital.

Hugh Garrison

Chapter 5

Negotiating with Yourself

How to negotiate the internal maze and remove conflict to better serve our customers and launch innovation is the vision we should strive to accomplish. The occasional Titan here is that every large, multinational company has to have boundaries—checks and balances with metrics that are driving the company to create equity among the functional organizations. The obvious example is that if we sold everything at cost, we would move lots of Widgets, but we would sadly go broke, being the volume only leader, with no balance to cost and margins. We could, of course, apply the theory that it's all about the technology and the next Widget. Again, without balance, we could have great intellectual property and no means to produce, market, or distribute the Magic Widget. The point is not to debate what the company's strategy is; the key takeaway is how we, as customer-facing leaders, manage the reality of the conflict of the internal organization, to accomplish our customers' goals in a way that is balanced with our company's directives.

The first step is to fully understand what functional groups affect and have a vote in the customers' relationship with the company. In a previous chapter, we visited the idea that the titles of the organizations outside our immediate span of control may vary; depending on industry, but it is the function they serve that we need to focus on. We need to appreciate what is driving our core business units; the teams responsible for the Profit and Loss of the company, is that market share or margin, unit growth, EPS or some combination of other market and financial metrics. To illustrate this, let's say the Magic Widget Company has eight main groups that get a vote in how

Hugh Garrison

the customer need is satisfied and we need to influence them to get things done for and with our customers. Think of a center circle—that's us—surrounded by other circles, containing functional groups such as finance, product development, executive management, program or engineering resources, legal teams, regional teams, marketing, and production.

Now that we've identified that part of the equation, we need to understand who the controls the overall decision. Chances are, in most matrix organizations, the functional groups control just what their name suggests. Finance or some derivative of product management controls the tactical pricing delegation and larger deal components that involve dollar aspects. Marketing is managing the brand and programs to promote awareness or adoption of specific Widgets. For each of these groups, we need to identify the control parameters and note their dependencies (or not) with the circle in our internal landscape. We shouldn't get caught up in what a perfect organizational fit would be or the politics of the people that run the groups. Regardless of organization titles, we need to know were and who is in the core groups within the company and we need to influence them to our cause.

With this organizational knowledge in mind, the image that should start to emerge is that the customer many times has a singular point of access for suppliers for a specific business event, whereas the internal machine requires multiple actions to affect the results. In essence, we spend a lot of time in a large organization negotiating with our own company, ourselves. Of course, this can lead to some frightening offshoots, if we lose sight of our role. Beyond general slow responsiveness to the market, we can become convinced that the internal metrics outweigh the customer's view. Of course,

Hugh Garrison

in reality, there is not a black or white answer; there has to be quest for balance. If we think of the classic scale analogy, on the one side is the value that the Magic Widget Company perceives, and the other side is comprised of the bag of gold the customer is willing to invest to get the value we have to offer. To be clear, depending on the situation, that value from the Magic Widget Company may be a service, patent, product, or technology. The bag of gold might be licensee agreements, money, share of business, or placement. The question that seems most omnipresent is, how do we negotiate with constancy across many internal groups, stay sane, and accomplish the original results we were aiming for to increase value to the customer? For starters, I would offer you what we talked about in chapter 2, when we briefly mentioned the concept that we can only negotiate internally with the delegation given by our customer.

For those of us in customer-facing leadership roles, the internal struggle of the Magic Widget Company, to embrace the value of what the customer is willing to invest for our solution, is the most challenging part of the job. This can tap into both our creative minds and our competitive spirits. We are, after all, very good stewards of the Magic Widget Company; we are tasked with the honor of representing the company to the g give the best advice and education about the Widget and how to manage the market. The good news is that the way to be both is through the same transparency we have already talked about.

As we combine the concepts we covered on transparency and created processes to educate the functional leadership on our customer and current status, we can move to the implementation phase. Our next steps are to start taking action to move our overall account strategy and vision forward.

Hugh Garrison

We will talk more on the strategic vision in future chapters; for now, let's stay engaged with the tactical concepts on how to span the chasm between our company's decision making process and getting to a mutual win.

As with previous examples, we will use very common ideas and put the focus on the concepts, instead of on the particular item or technology point. The example below will illustrate how a B2B relationship can get into troubled waters quickly over a seemingly straightforward request that has many implications and a path to smooth seas.

To best serve their markets, customers need to have insight into how our company designs the composition of our Magic blue Widget. The problem is, that is part of the Widget's "secret sauce." Just as important, this formula is protected by a patent and considered intellectual property of the Magic Widget Company—a Titan indeed. As we've developed credibility with our customers, as both a good steward of our company and a trusted advisor, we are now being asked how to handle this difficult request, so it will be resolved successfully.

Before you grab a ticket to headquarters or set up a video conference call with twenty-five people back in the legal group, we need to get to the delegation point from the customer that will allow us to carry their decision making authority to a specify criteria inside our company. . It starts with asking them what they are trying to accomplish. Why is the formula so critical to their success? What is the core of what they need? This is where we express that our open agenda is to help them accomplish their goal, but that we will need to be extremely clear internally as to why it is being asked, as we know the sensitivity around this formula is extremely high. Most of the time, what we'll find is that the original request came from somewhere outside our main relationship conduit's point of expertise They, like us, are trying to accomplish the right thing for their company—and they can't, without our help. The goal here is get to the core of what they need and not the peripheral request. As we explore the facts, we come to the mutual conclusion that what the customer actually needs is tied the base material used in the blue Widgets, so that they can build a solution around one specific part and need to understand any chemical reactions, not any Intellectual Property that is tied to our manufacturing process. Now that we have our delegation, success would look like the Magic Widget Company agreeing to disclose the material itself; this is more granular and possibly easier to solve than the original request. It doesn't mean we will get there, but it does mean we can now guide our company with other options or avenues to help the customer and also reach our own goals.

The next step is for the customer team or leader to come forward to the Magic Widget Company with a really tough request. Since we have already done the work to understand what each functional group is responsible for and the basics of who does what, we could conclude that there are three stakeholders: legal, product development, and executive branch. More than likely, it wont be a single call or meeting, as each of these groups has its own metrics and agendas, all of them aimed at making the Magic Widget Company successful and profitable. As we approach each group, we share our agenda and requests in a positive way. We are trying to find a path to help the customer understand our Magic Widget's blue formula; however, the recommendation is to first understand what we can and cannot tell them, and then go back with a united answer. It will be a similar routine with the other two groups as we build the end answer to the customer.

Hugh Garrison

Each group will present the reasons why they can or can not give the data asked for; that's OK, as we have already educated them that the customer wants to grow with us, not compete against us. Here is where we use our delegation point; as the three different groups discuss what can be done, we can coach them as to what the customer really wants (i.e., ensuring that by using our Magic blue Widget, their product does not turn green or orange). We must keep in mind, throughout this process, that our role is that of a facilitator, to help the internal group see why the customer wants what they do and the benefits to offering some level of support. Eight times out ten, we'll find middle ground with the functional teams. For example, perhaps they will agree to tell the customer what the materials are, but not the quantity of each material or the complete manufacturing process. Again, considering the original customer request, this is a compromise; to our delegation point, this is success. In those two times we can't reach an agreement that is what executive management is in the loop for. The premise is that we are engaged in Tier 1 accounts that are material to our company. This makes it necessary to ensure executive management is engaged. At this point, with the internal part near the end, you can state the delegation point and why the customer is requiring whatever the goal is. That can often tip the scales in some way, to allow more information or a delegation that will give us a win with the customer by looking at it from that angle. In our example, by giving them the minimum data on material, we don't sacrifice the secret sauce, and at the same time we ensure that our Widgets are designed for the customer's final solution, without compromise or concern. Whether we are talking about something technical, or something like business volume for a given price or license fee, the concept is that we have two negotiations. One is with the customer. And more times than not, the customer side will

Hugh Garrison

be about finding your delegation point. This will give you the critical knowledge of how you can be successful, either in gaining some level of business or a solution to a need they have. From this delegation point, we can now work the sometimes more difficult internal spectrum to achieve success. Keeping a balance for our company is very important and a very unique role we have as customer-facing leaders. It s easy to believe, within the four walls of the Magic Widget Company, that our product or service is truly Magical. By negotiating internally in a way that exposes the company to the larger business picture and then guiding them to the customer's delegation point, we ensure that the perspective of the collective organization incorporates a market and customer viewpoint. This valuable service we provide our company ensures that the "inside the four walls" thinking is overcome, and we can succeed in the greater market within our industry.

Major Points and Insight

To accomplish success at our customer, we must understand and be able to influence the internal machine that many times can take more effort than the actual customer negotiation.

As customer teams on B2B fronts, there are many functional groups we need in order to be successful with our customer and in turn deliver the results we are being measured. To do this we must fully understand what each functional group effects, controls, and holds the decision-making key that gives it a vote in the customers' solution with your company.

Determine what is the customer delegation point that means success for them and align that to the functional decision making processes, this will speed the process by acting as the customer decision maker.

Finding a balance to the decision and approach is critical; you are a steward of your company and counselor to the customer. Imbalance can't not survive long term, as it will change the other business elements to compensate and spinning the business slot machine and not always in your favor. Hence, find the path that creates value, balanced to both the customer and to the company you represent, that is were success lives.

Hugh Garrison

Chapter 6

Leadership: It Matters

How many books, training courses, and gurus have contributed to the topic of leadership? Just like you probably do, I try to read and absorb good leadership stories and techniques. Over the years, I've seen a lot of styles and approaches; I would honestly say there is not a Magic formula. However, it's clear where leadership is lacking and where it is being practiced. For our purposes, we want to identify some foundational leadership approaches to prevent leadership—and the lack of it—from becoming a Titan of contention.

From a B2B relationship management perspective, I believe there are three areas we have to focus our leadership efforts on: the customer, our support team, and inside the Magic Widget Company. Many times, leadership, or the act of leading, is predicated on basic fundamentals of communicating clear direction, consistent practices, and creating platforms to carry the vision forward. The cornerstone of leadership is the art of finding balance with decisions around our customers and internal objectives within the multidimensional and real-time business environment we operate in today's world of commercial commerce.

Customer

The customer will typically look to the sales leader for the Magic Widget Company's position of business posture, direction of the relationship, engagement expectations, and the trust layer. The other thing to consider is the business posture that exists between the companies. This is likened to the culture of the relationship; it is how things get done. From my experience, having an open posture and attempting to

Hugh Garrison

always provide the customer with choices when trying to solve problems or unlock opportunities is how growth and trust are encouraged.

As simple as this probably sounds, as many of us know from working between two large companies, there are many processes and metrics that act as concrete, rather than being the flexible conduit we need to create an open posture. There are several leadership techniques to craft this type of posture; one simple way is using the constructs in chapter 4 about transparency. The tactical actions is to proactively signal the customer leader to know what the driving metrics are for the Magic Widget Company and guide programs or business opportunities to those metrics to give them better chance for success. The first step is to acknowledge the request and open the dialogue, not to just use the creative killing word - "no." Chances are anyway that if the ERS (entire relationship spectrum = scope of business + your customer's size and scope) is large enough for the Magic Widget Company, the request or problem will get executive-level attention. More times than not, the expectation will be to have options for evaluation. From our work in Chapter 5 about "Negotiating with yourself", we know that establishing a customer delegation point around what they are trying to gain and how you can craft that to an objective for the Magic Widget Company is critical. While there won't be alignment every time and there will sometimes be a form of "no", when we always present an open posture and work to find common ground we'll move more forward than we do sideways or backward.

The last three remaining leadership roles to our customer (direction of the relationship, engagement expectations, and the trust layer.) can be aligned if we have the culture of the relationship set to an open posture. The direction can be linked to the overall vision; we look more at that in the following chapter. In essence, the overall vision for the partnership and the mutual identification of the 5 to 7 major imperatives that we choose to guide the engagements around and get the customer's buy-in that they are the right ones. This creates mutual ownership and a common platform to drive the business. Setting expectations is what helps build the trust layer around the relationship. These are the basic tenets of trusted expectation:

1) Do what you say you will, and don't commit to more than you can deliver.
2) If a message or data point is given in confidence, keep it that way. Always know that we are stewards of our company, so if we learn something that is material, we are obligated to make it visible. Tell the customer up front that that is what your intention is. Otherwise, use the data in a way to craft messages and align as you now have an insight.
3) Ensure that they know you will always ask clarification and seek their intent, before moving ahead with their message to the Magic Widget Company
4) This is a partnership, so make sure you treat it as such and include them in major decisions. With a focus on how each will communicate to the internal organization.

We made the case in chapter 3 that, like cars, teams have many moving parts; and if not all are working together in the same direction, it can cause some really disastrous effects. The larger and more complex the business partnership, the larger the team and process scope needed to manage it. If we apply that basic premise, the leadership foundation our team's need is built on clear direction for the customer service level, core metrics for the business, account strategy and the story internally on our relationship success with our customer.

Hugh Garrison

Support Teams

Leading global and/or extended teams can be challenging, as there can be both geographic and cross-functional differences. One simple way to begin the process of establishing transparent leadership is to establish a cadence of forums designed to have the customer team reporting out to the broader organization about the current state of the business and top issues being faced. It's this hallmark of constancy that builds the expectations and clear guidelines for the team that will have them performing at their best. The next step is to establish metrics that create common motion, followed by clear roles, so that each person knows what is expected and what he or she owes the team. Finally, we need to tie these to what we want on the relationship journey. The vantage point of the sales leader is a great place to not only see all the cross-functional points of the company, but also to engage with each one to represent the customer's vision. Depending on how your Magic Widget Company is aligned, you can set up regular 1x1with the counterpart in each of your support teams that does not directly report to you. For example, if Magic blue Widgets have to have daily deliveries to the customer in order to keep their business producing Widget-using devices, then the logistics leader is a person who definitely needs to understand the customer team's vision. It also establishes you as the go-to person for escalations and major events that affect your customer. We can delegate a team member to be the lead for a specific escalation event, however the critical part is that we create the escalation process and linkage back to the customer team.

When working with larger teams and expanded operations, it is a good idea to create a closed-circuit approach, allowing a continuous flow of current, as opposed to an open circuit,

Hugh Garrison

which does not allow the current to flow and connect points. Think of it as the relationship having a current flowing through it, just like a light switch does; the electricity is always flowing to it, but if the switch is off, the circuit is open, and the light will not come on. As our business flows events happen, positive events, like growth opportunities, and negative events, such as product or process issues. There are actions and deliverables that get created with either event cycle. However, if we don't have a defined process that brings back the closure to a forum or leadership view, the lessons of the outcome could be lost, or the timing could miss the mark. If the Magic Widget Company has a breach, and now a security issue has been found in the code, this constitutes an event. Now, as the solution is being determined, there needs to be a process that captures the actions and results to keep a formal database of the outcome and time to resolution. In this case, the closed circuit happens when the solution to the problem event is validated, ending in the notification of resolution and it's implementation. This could be applied to process issues well; the end goal is twofold. First, create awareness and closure to the issue through notification of the customer's team leaders. Second, create an ongoing knowledgebase that can be used by current and future teams to not repeat the same mistakes and for progressive learning. Once this knowledgebase is developed, you as the leader can use this to educate the wider organization and create a better team through your view of what works and what doesn't.

The Magic Widget Company

The last piece to the puzzle centers on our leadership of the customer team for the company, in this case, the Magic Widget Company. We as sales leaders play the critical role of translating the customer's world and needs in a meaningful way that our company can understand and take action to help

Hugh Garrison

solve those needs. As the sales leaders, we need to prevent the Titans of miscommunication and ensure that the market conditions that shape the customer environment are clear inside the Magic Widget Company. With the data points and structure we have already put in place throughout the book thus far, we can construct a customer briefing–type document and forum that includes our team structure, current goals, and top issues that need to be transmitted across the company. This might look like monthly communications calls with all the management team, functional leaders, and extended team to deliver the core strategy and continue the directional messaging. The core intent is really that we need to establish our team and ourselves as the customer leaders within the company. This comes from information sharing and direction on key events.

As the customer sales leader, we have a very unique holistic vantage point of the market through our customer's business, our company's view of products and market, and the internal functional team's perspective. With this expansive view, we have the responsibility and creative artistry to architect balance into events, communication, and solutions that allow both companies to find successful meaning. If our customer is asking for red Widgets, and our only line today is blue, and is costs four million dollars to set up a new line to produce, the balance may be in the deal structure. Perhaps the customer could get our red Widgets exclusively for twelve months, and we are able to charge a premium for our red Widget to fund the expansion. Hence, we gain long-term growth and diversity, the customer gains access to red Widgets, and we use the exclusivity for market growth.

Leadership, in all its various forms, through customers, teams, and company, needs to be taken into account as we work

Hugh Garrison

through the day-to-day customer relationship cycles. Structuring the business relationship posture or culture to an open one, you'll be able to successfully navigate the direction of the relationship, engagement expectations, and the trust layer. From a team level, through consistent metrics and forum cadence, we can build the expectations and clear guidelines for your team that will have them performing at their best. Then establish clear roles, so that each person knows what is expected and what he or she owes the team. Finally, we as the sales leaders can pull together the overall customer universe, leveraging this insight to enable balance through creating a platform to the larger company. by having a closed-circuit approach. This, combined with common metrics, functional group connections, closed-circuit approach, and broad communication, creates an environment for leadership to thrive.

Major Points and Insight

Being transparent in our leadership actions are critical to success when managing large B2B relationships as there are multitudes of supporting teams and stakeholders that need direction and information. This is predicated on the basic fundamentals of communicating clear direction, consistent practices, and creating platforms to carry the vision of our customer success journey inside our company and externally to the customer.

The cornerstone of B2B leadership is the art of finding balance between our company's objectives and the customer we are engaged.

There are three areas we have to focus our leadership efforts on to underpin the critical balance between the often competing objectives between two large companies; the

Hugh Garrison

customer, our support team, and inside the Magic Widget Company.

1) Customer leadership is based on the business posture we create, direction of the relationship, engagement expectations, and the trust layer. The direction of the relationship should be set by five to seven strategic imperatives that both you and your customer agree to create mutual ownership.

2) For the functional support teams we need to establish a cadence of forums designed to report out to them the current state of the business and top issues being faced by our company that are gating success with the customer. Creating a closed-circuit approach will allow for a continuous flow of current in the form of information as major events happen.

3) Inside the Magic Widget Company we have the responsibility and creative artistry to build balance into positive and negative events through our holistic vantage point, by communication methods and proposed solutions that allow both companies to find success.

Chapter 7

Creating the Vision

Up till now, it's been about the management of the relationship
and how to structure streamlined engagements. Now, we are
going to lift our gaze to look beyond the mechanics and see
the potential of what the relationship can be. Let's define what
we are after with this part of our blueprint. The vision, which is
about the long-term view of the customer relationship itself —
and in terms of business success, people on the team, and
market or product end state — needs to be like the banks of a
river. This analogy is that, like banks guiding the flow of the
water, our vision guides our strategy and tactics. For our uses,
the strategy will be how we accomplish our vision, and the
tactics are the tools we use to execute.

As we drop down through each of the components of the
vision, we should be underpinning these with the strategy we
need to accomplish. Not all of the elements of the strategy will
be in our control. That's OK; let's get them identified, and in
that way, we understand what is needed to complete our
vision. Some strategy or tactic elements are low risk, such as
pricing or supply. Others are more complex and may take
several stakeholders to reach support, such as product
development or technology access, legal or contract issues, or
far-reaching implications that might affect other parts of the
company beyond our customer relationship.

Vision is a subjective thing; in our business use, it is the act
and sometime art of seeing what can be, not limited to what
the present situation looks like (good or bad). Let's revisit our
basic tenets of CUSTOMER-TEAM-RELATIONSHIP-
MARKET-MECHANISM-PRODUCT to help us frame the

vision we want to create. It is important to have a vision, as it not only allows us some guiding influence, it gives you a beacon of the future. Something to keep focus on as the Titans we all face make their way in and out of our business relationship. You probably have an idea or instinct about what each of these needs to be and how they could look at their full potential. Your gut instincts created through experience are a great counselor and can be one source to determine if the path you're on feels right. In the sense of a time horizon of our strategy, we should be able to create a vision of what the business would look like in it's optimal and desired state going out six months to a year. Then we can build that out to create the same viewpoint for the next 2 to 3 years. These short and long term visions will help establish priorities, actions and resource needs for the tactical execution to achieve the optimal state.

I'd like to take us back to the three areas of customer relationship itself and in terms of business success, people on the team, and market or product end state and put our elements against them and see how we shape our vision.

Customer Relationship

As we discussed in chapter 1, customers typically see suppliers as part of the solution, pure commodity, or something they must control. If you're in one of those customer relationships where it is a struggle to achieve the tactical business objectives and create an island of unity, then your strategy may be to create a foundation of collaboration. This might look like setting three or four strategic meetings with the customer's core stakeholders, with the idea of bringing something new to the table; new market creation opportunities, joint development, or mutual agreement to a specific advantaged state of terms or access for some time

Hugh Garrison

period in return for volume or share assurances. The idea is that if you're in a difficult relationship, to have something that connects the companies on a deeper level than just the transactional relationship, so both leadership teams can commit to place the focus beyond the current cycle.

If you're fortunate enough to be at the helm of a mutually trusting business partnership, then you already have the foundation to create some great gains for both companies. The first thing you should do, as you might guess, is to sit down with your customer leader and define two types of goals. The first is clear progressive goals to continue to motivate the teams and showcase the success you have. These might be tailored to your market: maintain XX percent share or sustained joint development on the next-generation product and ten thousand user licenses per release, and so on. Document and outline the things that are making each of you successful so that you can both continue doing them with clear measures, and create standard process around them to help both companies replicate your great practices. Use this as a way to create altitude between the tactical business steps, such as cycle negotiations, and you can have your energy focused on growth and innovation.

The other type of goal you should create when you already have a successful relationship is one that is out of reach—a real stretch. This creates an environment of hyper competitiveness for your combined teams and gives you something to focus on above the day-to-day issues. Undoubtedly, crises and Titans of contention will rise up and your momentum may slow temporally. However, with your solid relationship and a distant horizon to stay focused on, the disruptions will subside and then return to the success pace.

Hugh Garrison

Business Success

We've talked about common metrics and measures to ensure everyone is on the same page regarding what the direction is—and to mark progress. As we define what business markers will equal success, such as four hundred million dollars in annual revenue or five million licenses of our Widget software sold, it's important that we have two sets: one for the internal company, and one we share with the customer. Of course, some can be the same; however, there are probably some internal measures around margin, cost, and Intellectual Property development that we want to keep inside the four walls.

We look at the market size and product and peer into the future of what it could be. Are there going to be developing countries that need blue Widgets, either in their natural state or as part of an integrated solution, from your customer? As we look internally, are there new types and attributes coming with future blue Widget releases over the next twelve to eighteen months that will open markets, customer avenues, or regions not now accessible? What are your company's business plans, geographic ambitions, and product development and market goals? These help shape our business success vision; for example, in eighteen months, Magic Widget Company, partnering with the Awesome Customer Company, will have four hundred million dollars in top-line revenue for the year, six new patents, expanded sales out in India and Brazil, and ten million Widgets sold at 40% standard margin.

Team Development

We looked at the importance of helping our many extended teams and some strategies that make us successful. Our vision needs to work around the concept that we want to

Hugh Garrison

enhance the team experience for our key members and bring our overall team performance to the next level. Take your strong leaders and give them extra assignments, preferably in their area of current responsibility. Remember the initial team assessment we did in the first part of the book? Those can be a good idea of where to start and develop your planning. This might take the shape of a salesperson leading or representing the team on an important internal project or an industry event. On a team level, maybe you want to have your whole team trained in a particular discipline or have them participate in a specific seminar or workshop. One idea is to have facilitators help with a Belbin Team Inventory, which is a personality test, designed to help define the traits of team members. There are other forms of personality tests as well. Through this investment in your team, you will not only gain powerful insight into your team (and they, in turn, will perform better through self) awareness), but the priority of the team's well being will also be very clear.

Market/Product End State

Assessing the Product, Mechanism, and Market elements is our foundation for the direction we want to take the vision around market/product end state. The construct is that we have products that align with the market goals of both companies. Although this will be industry specific, the basics will be similar. If we look at the Magic Widget Company, we see that they want to have the new purple Widget launch in eight months with their top customers. Being one of our top customers, Awesome Customer Company is a customer we need to be successful with. After meeting together, we determine that the new purple Widgets will allow the customer to compete in a new target market they need to grow in. Hence, our vision can take the form of new market access by our customer with our purple Widgets in eight months, with four million units over two quarters. As discussed, we are trying to create a view of a future state to help both companies guide the direction of the relationship and give something we can see above the fray of the sometimes-difficult days.

Once we have our internal and customer shared vision for success, we need to run for office. As with any large organization, public, private, or governmental, there are many competing demands for (usually) limited resources. Whether inside our own company or with our customers, being able to articulate our vision and strategy for success in a clear, easy-to-understand way is critical to getting all the resources you need.

Just like politicians of old, we should have a standard stump speech (vision + strategy) that we can incorporate into a five- to ten-page PowerPoint, Keynote, or our favorite presentation software. This is a package we would update every quarter, and which would be given to all major stakeholders, executives, and leaders to inform them about our business and the plans we have.

Some example of page titles for you to work with:
1. Current Customer Business Environment
   a. List the major account issues, competitive landscape, customer's financial statements and their goals/plans for the company's future in the larger market (typically found in their latest earning report if they are a public company)
2. Customer History and Projections
   a. Review basic financial metrics and those associated with your vision for the future
3. Customer Team Focus in FYXX
   a. Performance Measurement

Hugh Garrison

      b. Ensuring Team Success

      c. Celebrating Success

4. Five mutually supported imperatives

      a. List and depict the core initiatives supported by both companies and timing

5. Vision of Success

      a. Depict your vision in the major areas we've reviewed and the major strategies to underpin them

6. Foundation for Success

      a. Highlight core achievements

      b. Direction on building on to current

      c. Show Executive Alignment & Shared Vision of the Future with customer

7. Going forward—incremental pushes

      a. Give some strategy items that support your vision for the customer

8. Summary and outlook

      a. Summarize your top business success metric and largest need you have

      b. Ask for the help needed to reach the vision you have (might be more resources or budget approval for capital expenditures, etc.)

Just like the market swings, a vision needs to be reset, as the elements have significant changes. This process of developing a vision and the corresponding strategies to support them will allow you to step back and anticipate the potential Titans of contention before they arise. At the same time, making this a regular part of your sales cycle discipline, you will be able to have a clear, overarching picture of your business relationship, direction, and strategy needs at your fingertips. This, in turn, will give you good scope of what the direction needs to be to guide the day-to-day interactions and position for the future.

Major Points and Insight

To lead our company to success with our customer, we need to create a long-term vision of the customer relationship itself in terms of business success, people on the team, and market or product end state.

A successful vision guides our strategy and tactics. The strategy is how we accomplish our vision, and the tactics are the tools we use to execute it. To ensure we keep moving forward, sometimes we need to create altitude between the tactical business steps, such as cycle negotiations, and the need to focus on growth and innovation.

To enable clear understanding inside our company and rally the resources we need to accomplish our customer vision, we can incorporate our vision and strategy into a five- to ten-page presentation to present to the major stakeholders, executives, and leaders about our business and plans.

Just like the market swings, a vision needs to be reset periodically, as the elements have significant changes.

Hugh Garrison

Chapter 8

Pulling It All Together

We've covered much ground, from customer culture and competitive perspective to running for office in your own company, to ensure you get the right support through knowledge and awareness of the internal machine. From all of this, there are some common themes I'm sure you noticed. One of the core ideas is transparency in your interactions with the customer and your support foundation, through common metrics and open, consistent shared knowledge of performance and relationship status. Another key issue is time and the need for a vision beyond the current set of circumstances. If you can ensure the gaze is not always focused at the issues of the day-to-day, you can inspire a vision of what can be and, in so doing, set up the framework for the strategy elements this will naturally underpin. The other common thread is that there are cross-functional teams that support the range of activities between the companies. In that same theme, it is the role of the leader to ensure the right resource to the are being deployed to the right battle and scale the approach, so the experts can be allowed to do what they do best. Leadership is also the element that provides consistent direction and oversight to the holistic relationship. This all gets combined with the discipline of balance—balancing the needs and goals of the customer to the objectives of our company.

As we pull our relationship blueprint together, let's go back to the beginning and look at our business through the lenses of the B2B slot machine of situational variables. Below is a placeholder for you to identify the foundation; although not limited to these, it will help bring the current state into focus.

Hugh Garrison

CUSTOMER	TEAM	RELATIONSHIP	MARKET	MECHANISM	PRODUCT
Pro-Supplier	★ ★	Symbiotic	Open Market	★	Many Options
Market Leader		ERS = Workable	Unique Solution		
Open Culture	Customer Clash	Long-Term Plays	★	Understood Contract	Poor Quality
★	Internally Weak			Defined Process	Behind the Pack
	Disjointed	★ ★	Closed Market	Process Mapped	★ ★
Suppliers = Risk	★	ERS = Askew	Leader		
Titan		Conflict = Norm		★ ★	Only Solution
Internally Locked		Transactional		Add-Hock Processes	First Choice
★	Skills in Place		New Market Entry		
	Customer Trusted	★	High Entry Barrier	Exceptions are the Norm	Industry Leading
	Influencing Inside				

Now that we have our foundational understanding developed, we can pick the top areas we'd like to focus on to remove the Titans of contention through some of the techniques we have explored together. One area to explore is around the chance that the macro situation, economic, world or market event could spin? Although this is outside of the customer-supplier relationship, it can be powerful. For example, if there is a new material that is now available to make your Widgets at a lower cost, you could create a more cost-effective solution and open up more markets. A micro event, one that effects the supplier-customer but not the global or larger market and economy, would be that the overall demand for blue Widgets increasing three fold, creating a demand swing that puts an imbalance in the market. As we talked about, a state of imbalance cannot last forever; and during that time, the other pillars of the business will react to compensate. Your advantage will be that you see the situation for what it is and can create a longer-term vision that will use the current imbalance to start momentum. Then, as balance returns, you can benefit from the disruption. Put differently, if you realize the situation will at some point turn back to balance, you won't overreact in the short term and will be operating several steps ahead of the market. In addition, using the new material example, you might temporally increase your marketing and sales efforts to gain traction in the customer base. Simultaneously, you can be building the support structure for when the material cost becomes normalized and thus ensure a sustained revenue stream.

Remember, seeing the change that is taking place is the first step in acting upon an opportunity. Keeping your senses tuned to what is changing and how those changes will impact the other elements is critical to creating value for your company. The overriding principle is that balance will return, so treat these events as momentum makers, with a forward-looking interpretation of how the overall market will normalize and where the Magic Widget Company will want to be positioned.

Identifying the decision makers on each side of the equation is critical to understanding who to influence— and how—to get the outcome we need. As we discussed, beyond the procurement and sales organizations there are the profit and loss owners that will ultimately determine if we get the support we need to execute to our strategy. Furthermore, we need to determine the forums and cadence of engagement with these groups. We talked in chapter 7 about using a standard template to act as a tool to use where there is not a forum set, or if we are trying to educate the company about the customer to gain mind share internally The major topics and updates we want to include as a common update to use a "stump speech" of sorts include:

Hugh Garrison

1. Current Customer Business Environment
2. Customer History & Projections
3. Customer Team Focus in FYXX
4. Five Mutually Supported Imperatives
5. Vision of Success
6. Foundation for Success
7. Going Forward
8. Summary and Outlook

Below is a representation, on a small scale, of how to lay out the internal and customer engagement map to insure clear communication. This helps to establish time blocks and preparation discipline.

Magic Widget Co	Cadence /Forum	Last Review	Customer	Last Review
Finance	Quarterly Ops Review		Procurement organization	
Marketing	Monthly		New Product Launches	
Exec Management	Quarterly Biz Review		Semiannual Review	
Next Gen Core Team	Monthly		Joint Update Meetings	

As we have each of these interactions it creates a golden opportunity to express our vision and increase the awareness of the opportunities, risks, and needs of our customer relationship. The powerful thing about our vision is that it will give a glimpse of what can be, with the strategy we have developed around the tactics we will use. This act of transparency and information sharing will conquer the Titan of contention that lurks when functional groups and executives don't understand what is happening with large customers. In the void of information, scenarios and many times false assumptions are created. We should stay focused on ensuring our message, vision, and overall customer situation is communicated across the functional teams in a consistent cadence and format.

Teams make up the heart of the B2B interaction and success. Using the vision of how we want the overall relationship to be structured and the skill sets needed for the challenge, we can develop a template to start an evaluation of the direct and indirect teams. Through this evaluation of our teams' skill sets, behavior characteristics, interactions, and structure, we'll be able to make adjustments where needed and create a world-class team. As we manage through the ups and down of business, finding places that allow us to take our company's value and shaping that into something our customers can define as a core building block for their success can be the cause that can draw our teams' creativity.

Looking at our customers, we need to create a trust layer that will give us the most influence and delegation to be able to work internally and efficiently to get results. We can do this by setting an open posture and ensuring that we are running on common sets of imperatives to manage the business. We

Hugh Garrison

should focus on finding ways to create a culture of transparency and mutual success, versus short-term, one-sided wins. Once we have that positive culture, we can gain increasing delegation from the customer, to give us much more flexibility inside the Magic Widget Company to achieve mutual success. The advantage of B2B relationship management is that we can move across many functional organizations inside our company and at the customer to get a very unique view of all the moving parts that make the commerce engine move. As we develop standard guidelines for the normal business flow, we can expand our attention to what *can* be, thus creating a vision; and the strategies to support it will flow, as it will be clear what we're trying to accomplish.

Whether dealing with the customer, team, or company, thinking in terms of the time frame and adjusting our message to structure it to the future state can be a powerful way to see beyond any current Titan of contention. Any one of the issues—product, market, relationship, team, or even the customer or our company—can be the Titan, and it is not going to just go away. However, we can create a sense of common purpose and motivation to see options beyond the current state. If our business is moving and working in a forward direction, we can take that momentum to build a common bond across the relationship, to establish an agreed-upon execution model for the tactical business. If we can strive to create a common document and agreement that will govern the majority of repeatable business, it will allow for the focus to naturally fall back on the common strategy and innovation for the future. This, by its very nature, pushes the common dialogue to be about what *can* be and the strategies to underpin the future state.

Hugh Garrison

The optimum state for the B2B relationship is one of common direction, measure, and mutual profitability This state of an "arranged marriage," where we have companies engaged in a partnership of necessity and, typically, with an army of functional teams to manage, offers a vast opportunity for us to create lasting success. It isn't that Titans of contention won't arrive—they will—it is how we collaboratively deal with these challenges as customer and supplier. There will always be issues and gates to success when we have two businesses that are trying to mutually create value and, at the same time, produce individual profits. Facing these challenges with our customers and internal army will build strong bonds; and by leading with the principles we've talked about, we can bring out the best everyone has to offer. Being able to navigate the chasm between each company's independent strategy and finding the balance that allows a partnership to flourish and produce great results is the art the B2B selling. Understanding the pillars of the business relationships that expand and retract, based on the particular spin of the business elements slot machine, will allow us to see opportunities in the context of the total horizon. Taming the Titans that come our way, as we accomplish innovation and mutual revenue growth, is sometimes about applying the right perspective, principles, vision, strategy, and tactics that constantly move the momentum forward. I hope that the exploration of principles and looking from another vantage point will help you tame the Titans you might be experiencing, to give you a masterpiece B2B relationship.

Hugh Garrison